Little by Little

by
Ann marie Houghtailing

YELLOW ARROW
PUBLISHING

Baltimore, Maryland, USA

For my mother, who taught me to tackle life, little by little, and always find beauty in the quotidian.

Contents

LITTLE BY LITTLE

Uncooked Rice

My mother dug uncooked rice from my uncle's bloody knees
with tenderness and a safety pin

He kneeled on the rice holding rocks the size of cantaloupes
with arms outstretched
like a penitent

He and my mother were just hungry
so they went to the cemetery
making a hammock of their worn shirts
filling them with oranges and candies and nuts
that the Japanese had left on their loved ones' graves

The sugar plantation where my grandfather worked
did not provide enough to fill the bellies of four children and a wife

But hunger was not an excuse to steal
Uncooked rice was a form of punishment
Something so small and humble
meant to nourish you
can make you bleed and weep with shame

For me rice has always been a staple
we were taught to wash clean
before cooking in the rice cooker

My mother taught us to measure the water
using the lines on our middle finger

Didn't matter whose finger
the rice always came out the same
like it knew

The water would turn a cloudy milky gray
as you rinsed the hard pearly grains in your hands

Meat and vegetables over rice
Spam and rice
Beans and rice
Beans and rice again
when the time between paychecks stretched for miles

My mother tried to use rice as paste
when she was a small girl
to glue the bottoms of her hand-me-down shoes together
but the soles peeled away
making it hard to walk
She tried to fix them
to avoid the cruelty of children
who didn't necessarily have it better
but were happy to find someone
who had it worse

Standing at the kitchen window
I hold a fistful of clean rice
Its weight and texture as familiar
as my mother's hand

I close my eyes and I can feel
its history in my fist
food
punishment
a poor substitute for glue
a tradition
a staple
hard
and then soft

Nest

I placed too much hope
in the hummingbird's nest

I watched this vibrating emerald
place thready twigs and soft downy material
on a branch outside my window

I found myself holding my breath
during wild winds and unexpected rains

I underestimated her engineering skills
I exhaled
Good job mama

I needed her to triumph
I needed her to beat the odds
It was like a promise—an omen—a visitation

And then
something
something unseen
leveled her graceful home

The devastation revealed what I always knew

Love and diligence cannot protect
what is most precious

Safety is a lie
Sometimes luck is on our side
Sometimes it isn't
We need to endure
whatever unseen force may ravage our hearts

and we do
because what else is there?

Surrender

Surrender is not defined by war alone
Surrender is not a white flag
or knees in the mud
Surrender is not the beggar you think

Surrender is acceptance
It is the act of letting go

Death will come
It will take you
or worse still, someone you love
To surrender is to choose how you will let go

Surrender is accepting your suffering
with the knowledge that it cannot define you
but it belongs to you

You cannot smother the life from your suffering
Give it air and room to breathe
Be with it

Surrender is release
Liberation

It is not the reckless pleasure
of letting go of the wheel on a dark country road

Surrender is the conscious act of sitting in pain
watching my mother die and being still, not running
Or the courage to allow my children their mistakes
because there's beauty in those messes we all make

I've surrendered
not from weakness or foolishness
but from wisdom, wild courage
and a force of strength I did not know I possessed

The Cavalry Isn't Coming

By the time I was born
my parents were no longer together

I was the cost of free love in the '60s
My parents were beautiful and ill matched
my father a student at Cal
my mother 10 years his senior
with three teenagers

But for my arrival
my father would never have had children
I said this to him once over whiskey
and he said
"You were the very last thing I ever wanted
and the very best thing that ever happened to me"

I never lived with him
but he tells me when I was a baby without a crib
he would come over some evenings while I slept
He told me he used to rub my shoulders
between the barely-there blades of my infant body

He was growing wings
he told me he wanted me to have a large wingspan
to take me as far and high as I could go

My father told me to travel far and often
"No one ever laments the trip they took to Paris
At the end of a life no one wishes they had worked more"

He told me if I was ever to get down to my last $20
to blow it on a bottle of champagne
because at that point you might as well

"It's your world and I'm living in it"
That's what I said when a man pointed a gun at my 19-year-old body
and asked me to give him all of the money in the register
Those were my father's words
that he gave to me for just such an occasion

He also taught me to be a quitter
"I had a job when I got this one and I can get another one"
Don't accept disrespect or bad treatment
Not ever

He didn't tell me to say no to drugs or sex
He told me not to get drugs off the street
that if I wanted to try something I should come to him
He also told me that I didn't need to have sex in cars
he would give me the keys to his place and make sure not to be there

There were never jokes about keeping boys away from me
It was my body to enjoy and protect
He told me sex was my choice

My father didn't treat me like a princess
I had to saddle my own white horse
The cavalry was not coming

I've never called my father to solve a single problem
It wouldn't occur to me

My father never bought me a dress
or took me shopping for school clothes
but we spent hours in bookstores
and he never denied me a book

The Beginning Was The End

I was waiting for a train
You were waiting for something to happen

No matter how hard I try
I'm always running late,
    You said

I'm pathologically early,
    I replied

We would always be making a mess of things
Best we not bother,
    You suggested

And so it was all over before it began
But I have missed you madly ever since

Poetry

I wanted what you wanted
until we wanted different things

It turns out I'm no good at small talk
I prefer deep, muddy, messy talk
that takes place at kitchen tables and under the stars
late at night

I was starving all of the time
for poetry
and driving on dirt roads in search of old furniture

I remember
you held my naked feet in your lap
while I read poetry
and we were humbled and grateful for books
and below-average wine
and all of the gorgeous sentences we had yet to discover

Life got busier
and so noisy with small talk
at cocktail parties and barbecues
where no one discusses poetry
ever

Now you count calories
and steps
and measure your sleep and breath
hoping to delay death
not realizing that all this measuring is not a life
Did you learn nothing from Prufrock?

Feasting on Truth

I did not come with a spoon
to feed you

I came with a pen
to form words into sentences
to fill you up

I hid some sentences away
in drawers
and under cushions

So sometimes we could share silence
together

You said things in the dark
that you were too scared to say
in the yellow light of day

We did not need bread
nor butter
We feasted only on words
fat with truth
dripping with the warmth of breath

The Beautiful and Brief

Just like that
You took my baby boys
and made them men

When was their last skinned knee?

If only I had known
that the last time they called me Mommy
was the last time

I would have . . .
I would have . . .
held on?

Forgive me
I did not know
how beautiful
and brief it would be

Just let me catch my breath
the way my youngest son would catch butterflies
to touch their magic
before releasing them back into the world

Longing

You will wish for things
you can never have
things you didn't know you would yearn for

Not fancy cars
vacations or expensive jewelry

You will long for
forgiveness
better knees
one last hug from your mother

You will celebrate
things like birthdays
graduations and marathons

When it's the humble struggles
that nearly broke you

No one buys you champagne
for raising a teenager
helping your parents die
or surviving heartbreak or job loss

You will give up your dream of living in a villa in Italy
or a pied-à-terre in Paris

Your new dreams will be about having enough
Having enough will become wildly luxurious
enough time
enough freedom
enough healthy days
deep talks and long hugs

You will long for enough
and wonder how you could have ever wanted more
when enough was everything

Porch Pirate

Dear Porch Pirate,

As you can see, I've made this box for you. There's food and a few other things, although probably not the electronics you were hoping for. I've lived in this house for over 20 years, and no one has ever taken anything from me. That is until you stole two packages off my front porch.

I'm so sad that you felt you had to do this because it means you must be in a bad place. I'm in a bad place, too, Pirate. Four members of my family have died in the last year. My brother-in-law, whom I've known my whole life, died right before Christmas. My mother died in August, just on the other side of this front door.

You know what I order from Amazon. You know that my dear friend sent me Joan Didion's book, *A Year of Magical Thinking*. I've read it before, but I would like to have the note that accompanied it. So you should know who you're stealing from.

I think you're male. Maybe that's a sexist assumption. Women can do anything that men can do, but when I think about taking a package from the front door of a very busy street, I assume you must be a young man. I wonder if you're on drugs. I hope you're not. My brother was an addict. I saw him about a year before he died. He told me he was clean, and he also told me about how he used to run around with a 9mm trafficking drugs and how he carjacked a woman once. He was killed in a motorcycle accident in September of last year.

Pirate, every morning I place my hand on my heart and say, "Good morning," out loud to myself because I will never hear my mother say those words to me ever again. I close my eyes so I can see her face. Last weekend for the first time in my entire life I spent 24 hours in bed. I didn't read or watch television or look at my phone. I was just still and silent. That was the day you took all of my packages. I miss my mother terribly. She loved me like no one else ever could.

I hope someone loves you that way. I hope someone misses you when you're away from them and worries about your well-being. I'm worried about you, Pirate. I'm worried you're going to do things that are more dangerous than stealing packages. I've been inside of a men's prison many times. It's not a way for a human to live. I worry that someone will catch you and beat the hell out of you. That's what would have happened to you where I grew up. No one would have cared if you were hungry or desperate or addicted because they for sure had been in one of those states at one time or another.

I've seen many videos of people stealing packages. Even the news runs these stories. Naming and shaming is a blood sport now. I cringe every time I see one of these videos. I would never leave you a dead rat or chase after you or try to hurt you. That wasn't always the case. But I think all my youthful rage has died with all the people I love. Now I ask myself, "What would love do?" I've been tough my entire life. It's a lot of work to make sure you don't become hard.

There's a saying that goes something like, "We're all liberal and compassionate until they breach the garden gate." Well, the gate has been breached, and I am here, Pirate. So don't run. Come closer. Write back to me. If you do, I promise to keep leaving letters for you. You can tell me anything. It's easy to take, but try doing something really hard. Leave something on my porch. Leave a piece of yourself. I bet you don't trust anyone, and I understand that. Trust is a complicated business, and frankly, I'm not so great at it either. But you can't have love without trust. Tell me how you live. Tell me about your parents. I want to know how old you are and what sort of things you daydream about. You know a lot about me. You know my name, my address, and that I needed a new document shredder. Do something wildly brave and tell me who you are. I left you some paper and pen so you can write to me. Stick the letter in the box so it doesn't blow away.

I'm not delusional. I know that I can't save you anymore than someone can save me. We're all in our own fight. We have to keep our gloves up, our feet moving, and our head out of the way. But if we're very lucky, there will be someone in our corner cheering us on, rubbing our shoulders, giving us water, and reminding us that we are stronger than we think. Who's in your corner, Pirate?

I think you're lost, Pirate. It's okay. I'm lost, too. I know without knowing you that you're broken, because we're all broken. It's hard to love yourself. Harder still if no one loves you. I think about the way my mother loved me or the way I love my children with wild abandon, without judgment. That's how we should all love ourselves. I think that kind of love is a human right.

You know what a lot of people don't understand? Heartbreak doesn't actually kill you. Everyday I open my eyes and I think, I'm still here. It's remarkable. I've decided your thieving was a gift. This is what I do now. I tell myself that inside of every terrible thing is a gift. So in a way, I'm telling you that you're a gift.

I'll be waiting to hear from you. Until then, take good care of yourself.

In love,
Ann marie

The Suffering Place

No one can ameliorate your suffering
It's all yours

I can only sit inside of your suffering with you
and so I will sit low to the ground
where your sorrow seeps into the earth
through cracks made by your rage

I will let your heart beat like an ancient drum
and let you feel the suffering place
that can feel like an ocean with no horizon

You may want to run
but I invite you to stay

Be with your suffering
There is a kind of savage comfort there
for no other reason than it is truth

What would happen
if you released the animal howl of your agony?
Where would it go if you liberated it
from your innards?

Open your mouth
wide and wider still
and howl

Let your bones vibrate with the force of your suffering
Wail
Let your ears bleed with the sound of your own voice
The voice you did not know was yours

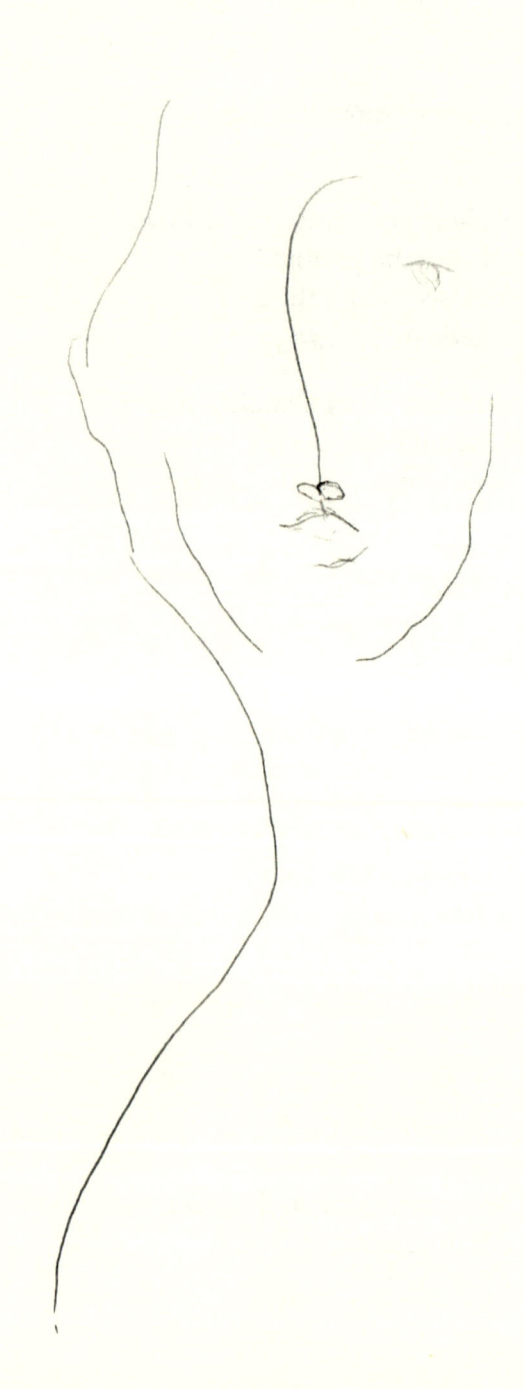

Like Me

I know about the small nick in your tongue
near your right back molar

I know how that nick was created

Be nice
be likable

You swallowed this belief thinking it was a vitamin
but it was a drug
a drug that made you sick

That made truth retreat
and your voice so small
it can't be heard by the human ear
not even your own

You were such a dutiful girl
head down
work hard
don't complain

No one told you
you can't make an impact
you can't make change
and
be liked

No one likes a truth teller

You're trying to stop taking the drug
but coming down is hard

Likability with a nice-girl chaser
has been your cocktail for so so very long

You tremble with the fear of the unknown
sweating the drug from your pores
feeling the tingle of being that woman
The unlikable troublemaker

What will it mean?

It will mean
you are free

Tell the truth
straighten your spine
so the little girls behind you don't have to be drugged like you

They will tell you
"You catch more bees with honey"
Tell them you're allergic to bees

Stop Apologizing

I know
it hurts not to be liked
They designed it that way
so you would be dependent, unsure and always other focused

What no one tells you is
that when you stop worrying about being liked
you can truly be loved
You can save yourself and all of the others

And are you liked, by the way?
Or is your compliance just appreciated?

You have unlikable women to thank
for all of the freedoms you enjoy

Women who said, "No, not on my watch"

Likability can be a useful tool
when you know how to employ it
but be careful
Its intent was self-immolation

You ask
"Can't I be liked and make change?"
No one has yet

"Will it be painful to stop taking the poison?"
Yes, my love

It will fill you with fear
So much fear
But then
Then you'll be free

Perfect

She wore a cape
and a tutu
and light-up sneakers
and a crown
and a smile as wide as possibility

She walked through the airport
like she owned it

She couldn't have been more than five

She was filled with confidence
and purpose
and certainty about her place in the world

I stood behind her and her mama at the café
I looked down at her and said, "Hello"
and she looked me in the eye and boomed, "HELLO!"

She thought she was perfect

I turned from her with my black coffee and heavy heart
and I cried wild, uncontrollable tears
fat, hot, and salty
with knowing

Knowing she would be poisoned
every day
a little at a time
but never enough to kill her

Just enough to make her sick

Enough to make her question her perfection
Enough to erase her and replace her

With a woman who would be told
You're too much
and eventually
you're not enough

I cried because I was perfect, too
Once
A long time ago
before the poison spilled from all those mouths
into my small, soft ears
and made their way into my blood
and bones
and brain

We were all perfect once

Parentified

I was a child
but not for very long
just nine glorious years

Then my sister died
and the universe shifted

My gentle, single mother
who had always made me
the center of her world
disappeared

I was replaced
by grief in one swift blow

The day she made the animal sound
a mother makes when she loses a child

Grief moved in
Grief was a ravenous brute
feasting night and day

In the twitch of a hummingbird's wing
I became an adult

Death is a rite of passage
the beginning and the end

To be parentified
is to lose your innocence
and taste cruelty
like a piece of rotten fruit

I learned to swallow
oceans of tears without drowning

My mother did
her very best
to stay on this planet

The death of my sister grew me up

I would forever be
my own caretaker

In the rare moments anyone tried to help me
I ran like a hunted rabbit

I could not trust such tenderness
knowing it could be torn from me
with wild violence

I had learned not to disturb
my mother's bleeding heart
with my own needs

There was simply
no room

I learned to need less
and less
until I needed nothing
I asked for nothing

And always, always
made space for others'
pain and struggle and sorrow
forever and ever
until I became
strong

Strong means
you never inconvenience anyone
with your needs

Strong means
you do not evoke sympathy
that's reserved for those
not as strong

Strong is a little girl
dressed in a power suit
aching to be fragile
hungry for the taste of comfort
starving for a moment
of unabashed, glorious, savage,
weakness

How to Mend a Wound

I filled my wounds with dirt from the garden
and dressed them with heavy paint
applied in brutally bold colors on a sanitary white canvas

Words were good, too
I placed them in gaping holes
I ate them like medicine
I wrapped them around me like a sacred blanket

Healing didn't find me in a reclined position
on a chaise lounge

Healing was located in the garden
where I got close to the ground to remove weeds
amend
and plant

My wounds were knitted together
with sentences waiting to be read
or written

And paint that I applied
with my fingers
because I could not bear
the distance a brush would create
between me and all of that white space

And miles of walking
going nowhere in particular

All of it together
was necessary

Wounds are tender
They take time
be patient
Give them lots of air
and light
and words
and paint
and dirt

I Will

I sit with the old
the demented
and the dying

Sometimes they time travel
Sometimes they transport to another place
Sometimes they turn me into someone they knew
before I was even born

I have learned to follow
I go into the forest
or back to Cleveland
or out on a date in 1946

I sit
I listen
I follow

Yes I see the rabbit in the corner
It does smell like lavender in here
I love traveling by train as well

Surrendering to now is a kind of promise

I will rock in the cradle of sorrow with you
I will stand in the darkness until morning with you
I will go back and back and back to a place I've never been with you

I will follow your lead as you make your way to the end of this place
and bid you a safe merciful journey

How to Apologize

First
set down your shield

If your sword is nearby
throw that as far away as you can

Now get low to the ground

Listen

Not just with your ears

Listen with your eyes
and your skin
and your organs
as if you are about to pet a feral mother cat

Breathe

Listen some more

Now look in the eyes
of the wounded

This will be hard

Now you can speak

Say thank you
for telling me
You are brave my darling
I am so sorry that I harmed you

You have a right to your pain

I hope you will forgive me
I promise I will be a student of this moment
I will strive to be better
please be patient
I'm human

The Whisper

The hot, wet whisper of death
is always on my neck

It came into the world with me
I almost died before I took my first breath
They thought my mother would die, too

Instead I howled
my arrival into the world
with a pink fist raised in rebellion

My grandmother died too young of a terrible disease
that would take half of her children, too
My aunt lost five of her six children
before she died
Suffering is not equitable

My mother was lucky
She didn't have any of those wicked genes
but she lost half of her children before she died, anyway

And

My brother lost his first son
My sister lost her only son

Her only son lost his first child

I am the only one of my siblings
alive with no dead children
That whisper is thick and heavy on my neck

It burns so hot
and then goes cold

Always

I have to choose joy
that stands against the wall
like the kid least likely to be picked
in gym class
looking at her shoes
casting a spell of invisibility

Don't believe what they tell you
you can't buy joy in a new car
It's not basking in the sun
of a white, sandy beach

It's you
rising out of bed
tasting coffee
not drinking it
but tasting it

It's you resting
in the quiet of a perfect sentence
on a Sunday

Peeling an orange
soaking in a bath
writing a note

And digging weeds out of the earth
and planting something in their place

Close Like That

We don't go on weekend getaways together
Sometimes we don't even speak on holidays
We aren't close like that

We don't even look like sisters

My sister braided my fine baby chick hair into submission
My scalp was hot with her brushing and taming
My barely there baby chick hair was not like hers
Thick, black, and coarse like ground pepper

My sister tells me I saved her
She never says from what
She doesn't have to

My sister learned words just so she could teach them to me
She wanted me to be better
As if there was a finite amount of confidence in the world
She sacrificed her portion
and put words into my mouth with her long, brown fingers
"Eat, eat," she said, nourishing me

She couldn't have been more than 17
Holding me on her hip at the Pussycat Theater in Oakland
picking up food money from my mom's best friend
while my mother was working at one of her
many, many menial jobs to keep
us all alive

We're a different kind of close
The kind that watched my mother howl like a trapped animal
when our sister died
The kind that ached over our brother's life filled
with drugs, violence, begging, suicide threats,
homelessness, and finally
death

I needed my brother to outlive my mother
a little grace she had certainly earned
but that was a hope too great for our kind

We are my mother's sole surviving children
We're close like that

My sister calls me in Portugal
where I am celebrating my 50th year of life
She tells me our brother's dead
My sister's only son died just four months ago at 44
now she must go tell my mother her only son died, too

In another 11 months we will sing our mother out of this world
and into the next
and four months after that
my sister will say goodbye to her husband
a man I knew all my life
a man I called brother

We're close like that

My sister probably looks like a normal person
She's not
Never was
Never will be

Son, brother, mother, husband
gone in a matter of months
and there are others from before
sister, granddaughter, nephew
Have I left anyone out?

Normal is not possible you see

When I return from Portugal
together we crawl into my bed
My sister, 65, holds me, 50, in her arms
and we ask ourselves
Who is next?

I win
It was my mother
She loses
Her husband follows my mother

That's the kind of close we are

Human Mothers

The boy,
I call him a boy, but he's a young man,
acts as if his anger toward his mother is original
It's his rage so it must be precious

I tell him I loved my mother
She's dead now
No one will love me or see me the way she did ever again

I tell him I used to want a different mother, too,
because I didn't always see my mother
I saw that part of her that refused to go to the dentist
when she got an infection
and eventually lost all of her teeth

I wanted a mother who could afford to go to the dentist

I wanted a mother
who didn't love a man who tried to strangle her
in front of me
We're all wanting something

One day all the fog of my dewy, entitled, youthful rage lifted
and I saw a woman
a woman who fought like hell for every scrap she got
a woman who was pursued by lots of men
a woman who had been loved
nearly to death by the men in her life

All that wanting got replaced with devotion

My mother loved me
she's why I'm alive
not just why I was born

I don't know what crime your mother committed, boy
It might have been truly terrible
Mothers are just people after all
and some people are truly terrible
because they don't know how to be in the world

But if she's just human
if she just wasn't what you ordered
then make sure the punishment fits the crime

Mothers are people with complex histories, dear broken boy
They have desires
Heartache
Great sex and bad sex
Pink and gold dreams
And deep invisible scars in places you can't see
that were made before you made your mouth into an O
and screamed your first wet cry into the world

Fall in Love With Your Wristbone

Clear the debris of others' opinions
from your lens
Clean away the pollution of the thoughts that work
like violence against you
Stop eating the poison of cruelty
which comes from a person who is broken
in ways you cannot see

Start with something small
Fall in love with your wristbone
See how it reminds you of your grandmother?

The feet that you thought ugly
are your father's that help you stand straight and proud
They are beautiful

Love yourself
Speak to yourself with the kind of tenderness
you would whisper to a baby you were rocking to sleep

Forgive yourself
Forgive yourself the way you would forgive someone
you love deeply

Place the palm of your warm hand
on your naked heart
and remind yourself that you are worthy of breath
Breathe
Eat the sunlight and chew on the stars
and let go of that which does not nourish your precious being

Little by Little

Little by little
my mother would say
when life was too slow for me

Little by little she would say
when I was trying to crawl
my way out
of
frustration
heartbreak
debt
disappointment or failure

Even the wisdom was small
Three words
you could fit into the palm of your hand

Or on matching metal bracelets
that I bought one Mother's Day
one for me
one for her

Little by little
is how I've survived the loss of her
and those that went before her
and after

Little by little is how I've learned to breathe again
pick up a pen
a paintbrush
stand on wobbly legs that wanted to collapse

Little by little
I whisper under my breath
day in
and day out like a heartbeat
My mother's voice
still sitting in my ear

Acknowledgments

There are so many people to thank for making me brave and making me better. There are teachers, friends, family, and strangers who have given me courage. I'm grateful to my mother who gave me a corner in our tiny apartment where I could think and write. I have my eldest sister, Sharolyn, to thank for all the vocabulary she intentionally learned so she could feed me words. I'm grateful to my father who spent hours taking me to bookstores all over the Bay Area.

I want to extend my gratitude to my sons who are full of kindness and encouragement and have borne the weight of a less-than-typical mother with grace and humor.

Deep thanks to Candace Walsh who has been a great mentor, coach, and champion of my writing. Special thanks to Leah Singer who has been on the writing road with me for many, many miles up mountains and down ravines and into the heart of truth. I'm grateful to Tanya Taylor Rubinstein for always reminding me that I'm a writer. Thank you, Michelle Baker, for always showing up with an open, generous heart and clapping the loudest. A big thank you to my business partner, Holly Amaya, who cheers me on and celebrates all my wild ideas. Thank you, Linh Tang, for all the years of investing in me, and to Eva Kwong and Amanda Allen who showed up in my darkest hour of grief and wrapped me in kindness. Thank you, Deanne Steele, for all the dinners and the space to grieve. Thank you, Frann Setzer, for being the best travel partner and plus one. And Karen Van Dyke, thank you for everything; I miss you dearly.

I also want to thank Paul Padgett for helping me manage the files for the cover and interior art, and Stephen Serieka who has been a loyal friend, constant champion, and compassionate witness through the years.

Finally, thank you, Yellow Arrow Publishing Editor-in-Chief, Kapua Iao, and her entire team. I so appreciate Ann Quinn's edits on one poem in particular that made the work richer and stronger. Thank you to Melissa Nunez for the lovely conversation, and Alexa Laharty for the design work. It's been a privilege to collaborate with all of you. Other members of the Yellow Arrow team include executive director Annie Marhefka; editors Angela Firman, Meg Gamble, Leticia Priebe Rocha, and Beck Snyder; intern Jacqueline Goldman; and the author support team, Marylou Fusco and Gabby Granillo. I'm sure there are many more invisible contributors who made this publication possible. For those I have not named, I tip my hat to you.

Ann marie Houghtailing has a graduate's degree (ALM) in American literature from Harvard University Extension. She has delivered a TEDx Talk entitled *Raising Humans,* and performed her critically acclaimed one woman show, *Renegade Princess,* in New York, Chicago, Santa Fe, San Francisco, and San Diego. Houghtailing is a visual artist and cofounder of the firm Story Imprinting. Her writing has appeared in the *Washington Post, Huffington Post, Daily Worth, XO Jane, San Diego Business Journal,* Yahoo! Finance, and *Thought Catalog.*

Thank you for supporting independent publishing.

Yellow Arrow Publishing is a nonprofit supporting writers and artists identifying as women. Visit YellowArrowPublishing.com for information on our publications, workshops, and writing opportunities.